Little Pebble™

Baby Animals and Their Homes

BABY ANIMALS In BURROWS

by Martha E. H. Rustad

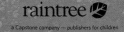

raintree

a Capstone company — publishers for children

Raintree is an imprint of Capstone Global Library Limited, a company incorporated in England and Wales having its registered office at 264 Banbury Road, Oxford, OX2 7DY – Registered company number: 6695582

www.raintree.co.uk
myorders@raintree.co.uk

Editorial Credits
Carrie Braulick Sheely, editor; Juliette Peters, designer;
Tracey Engel, media researcher; Katy LaVigne, production specialist

ISBN 978 1 4747 3331 1 (hardback)
20 19 18 17 16
10 9 8 7 6 5 4 3 2 1

British Library Cataloguing in Publication Data
A full catalogue record for this book is available from the British Library.

Acknowledgements
We would like to thank the following for permission to reproduce photographs: Alamy: Mark Colombus, 7, NatPar Collection, 20–21; Minden Pictures: Konrad Wothe, 19; Na-ture in Stock/Ronald Stiefelhagen, 9; Shutterstock: Henk Bentlage, 13, 15, HHsu, 11, ifong, Back Cover and Design Element, Michael C. Gray, Front Cover, Ondrej Prosicky, 3 Bottom Left, sittipong, Back Cover Design Element, Vladimir Wrangel, 5, Volodymyr Burdiak, 1 Bot-tom Left, Waddell Images, 17

Every effort has been made to contact copyright holders of material reproduced in this book. Any omissions will be rectified in subsequent printings if notice is given to the publisher.

All the Internet addresses (URLs) given in this book were valid at the time of going to press. However, due to the dynamic nature of the Internet, some addresses may have changed, or sites may have changed or ceased to exist since publication. While the author and publisher regret any inconvenience this may cause readers, no responsibility for any such changes can be accepted by either the author or the publisher. Printed and bound in China.

Contents

Burrow babies

Some baby animals
grow up in burrows.
Burrows are
under the ground.

A puffin chick lives in the back of a burrow. **Cheep!** Its parents feed it fish.

Zzz.

A badger cub sleeps.

It wakes up.

It drinks milk from mum.

Baby rabbits need a home.

A rabbit digs a burrow.

She lines it with fur.

Up and down

Prairie dog burrows are big.

Pups grow in one room.

They come up to play.

Baby meerkats look out.

Bark!

Mum warns her pups.

They go back down.

A baby armadillo

looks for food.

Mum helps.

They find some beetles.

They go back in their burrow.

A trapdoor spider looks out.

A bird!

She closes the door.

Her babies stay safe.

Eggs lie in a burrow.

Crack!

Baby desert tortoises crawl out. Hello!

21

Glossary

armadillo a desert animal with bony plates covering its body

burrow a hole in the ground made or used by an animal

parent a mother or a father

tortoise a reptile with a hard shell

warn to tell about a danger that might happen

Read more

Animals That Dig (Adapted to Survive), Angela Royston (Raintree, 2014)

Inside Rabbit Burrows (Inside Animal Homes), Liz Chung (PowerKids Press, 2016)

Look Inside a Burrow (Look Inside), Richard Spilsbury (Raintree, 2013)

Websites

www.bbc.co.uk/nature/23632577
See photos of animal burrows and learn how to identify which animal made them.

www.bbc.co.uk/nature/life/European_Badger
Learn more about how badgers live, and view videos of badgers.

Comprehension questions

1. How do burrows help keep baby animals safe?

2. Look at the photo on page 17. How do you think the bony plates on the armadillos help to protect them?

Index